W9-ASC-079

DATE DUE

781.66
KEN

Kenney, Karen Latchana
Cool rock music

$18.95
BC#32457105001113

DATE DUE	BORROWER'S NAME

781.66
KEN

BC#32457105001113 $18.95

Kenney, Karen Latchana
Cool rock music

Morrill ES
Chicago Public Schools
6011 S Rockwell St.
Chicago, IL 60629

Cool
ROCK
MUSIC

Create & Appreciate What Makes Music Great!

Karen Latchana Kenney

ABDO Publishing Company

Visit us at www.abdopublishing.com

Published by ABDO Publishing Company, 8000 West 78th Street, Edina, Minnesota 55439. Copyright © 2008 by Abdo Consulting Group, Inc. International copyrights reserved in all countries. No part of this book may be reproduced in any form without written permission from the publisher. The Checkerboard Library™ is a trademark and logo of ABDO Publishing Company.

Printed in the United States.

Design and Production: Mighty Media, Inc.
Photo Credits: Anders Hanson, Photodisc, Shutterstock
Series Editor: Pam Price

The following manufacturers/names appearing in this book are trademarks:
ACE$_{SM}$ Hardware, The Paintin' Place®, Organic Valley™

Library of Congress Cataloging-in-Publication Data

Kenney, Karen Latchana.
  Cool rock music : create & appreciate what makes music great! / Karen Latchana Kenney.
     p. cm. -- (Cool music)
  Includes index.
  ISBN 978-1-59928-974-8
  1. Rock music--History and criticism--Juvenile literature. 2. Rock music--Instruction and study--Juvenile. I. Title.
  ML3534.K45 2008
  781.66--dc22
                          2007038169

Note to Adult Helpers

Some activities in this book require the help of an adult. An adult should closely monitor any use of a sharp object, such as a utility knife, or perform that task for the child.

Contents

The Music Around You

Did you ever get a song stuck in your head? Maybe you just couldn't help singing it out loud. Sometimes a song reminds you of a day with your friends or a fun vacation. Other times a tune may stay in your mind just because you like it so much. Listening to music can be fun and memorable for everyone.

We hear music everywhere we go. Music is played on television shows and commercials. There are even television stations dedicated to music.

Most radio stations play one type, or **genre**, of music. Some play only country music. Others play just classical music. Still others play a mixture of different kinds of rock music. Just pick a kind of music that you like, and you will find a radio station that plays it!

The different genres of music have many things in common, though. They all use instruments. Some instruments are played in many different types of music. The differences are in the ways instruments are played. For example, the drumbeats are different in various music genres.

Some kinds of music have **lyrics** that are sung by singers. Did you know that the human voice is often referred to as an instrument?

Playing music can be as fun as listening to it! Every person can play a part in a song. You can start with something simple, such as a tambourine. You could then work your way up to a more difficult instrument, such as a drum set. Remember, every great musician was once a beginner. It takes practice and time to learn how to play an instrument.

With music, one of the most important things is to have fun! You can dance to it, play it, or listen to it. Find your own musical style and make it your own!

A Mini Musical Glossary

classical music – a type of music from Europe that began centuries ago as the first written church music. Today it includes operas and music played by orchestras.

country music – a style of music that came from the rural parts of the southern United States. It is based on folk, gospel, and blues music.

hip-hop music – a style of music originally from New York City in which someone raps lyrics while a DJ plays or creates an instrumental track.

Latin music – a genre of music that includes several styles of music from Latin America. It is influenced by African, European, and native musical styles. Songs may be sung in Spanish, Portuguese, or Latin-based Creole.

reggae music – a type of music that came from Jamaica in the 1960s. It is based on African and Caribbean music and American rhythm and blues.

rock music – a genre of music that became popular in the 1950s. It is based on country music and rhythm-and-blues styles.

The Rock Story

It's that rock beat that makes you want to move! Did you know that the rock beat came from African music? Rock music has grown from that beat, however. Electric guitars and a fast **tempo** changed the music. Since its beginnings, rock music has experienced some important changes.

Mid-1800s to early 1900s. Blues music began in the cotton fields of the southern United States. Slaves sang to each other while working in the fields. Their songs had the rhythms of Africa and told sad stories about life. Their **lyrics** were improvised and repeated in verses. Later, blues music was played with **acoustic** guitars.

1940s. R & B became very popular in Chicago. Muddy Waters and Chester "Howlin' Wolf" Burnett are two talented and popular R & B musicians associated with this period.

1930

1940

1950

1930s. Blues musicians moved to cities in the north. The music started to change. Musicians began playing electric guitars. The songs started sounding more fun and energetic. This electrified blues is called rhythm and blues (R & B).

1950s. New wild and energetic R & B performers appeared. Little Richard shouted his vocals and his music was fast. Chuck Berry mixed country music with a boogie-woogie beat. The beat made the music fast and fun for dancing. This new music was rock and roll!

1954. A new musician named Elvis Presley showed up in Memphis, Tennessee. He appeared on popular television shows. Americans saw Elvis perform as the TV **audiences** went wild. People loved Elvis, "the King of Rock and Roll."

1980s to 1990s. Grunge music arrived on the rock music scene. The grunge sound has distorted guitars and heavy drumming. Nirvana and Pearl Jam are two bands that made this music popular.

Late 1960s. The electric guitar became a bigger part of rock music. Jimi Hendrix and Eric Clapton played a new kind of electric blues using guitar effects. Heavy metal also grew from the blues. It was a loud and explosive-sounding music. The bands Led Zeppelin and Black Sabbath first made this music popular.

1960

1970

1980

1970s. Punk rock became popular. This music is very fast and loud. The Clash and the Ramones are two early punk rock bands.

Early 1960s. England became part of the rock-and-roll scene. The Beatles idolized Elvis Presley and played similar songs in their early music. They were the first of many bands that were part of the British Invasion of American rock and roll.

There are many variations of rock music. Each new rock band is influenced by the sounds of other bands. But, while rock music changes, that steady rock beat remains the same!

What Is Rock Music?

Rock music sounds great, but how is it made? Music has some basic elements, which are rhythm, **lyrics**, group formation, and song composition. What makes each of these elements specific to rock music?

The Rock Rhythm

Rock music is heavily based on rhythm. The rock beat usually has a 4/4 rhythm. This means that the beats are counted out in sets of four. A rock rhythm emphasizes the backbeat. The backbeat is the second beat and the fourth beat in a four-beat rhythm.

Lyrics

There isn't a certain style of lyrics used just for rock music. Songwriters write about their emotions or a single important moment. Sometimes they tell a story or voice a political belief through their lyrics. Rock lyrics are about anything you could think of in life.

Who's Who in a Rock Group

A typical rock group usually consists of four to five people.

DRUMMER

LEAD GUITAR

LEAD SINGER

BASSIST

Song Composition

Rock songs usually contain three parts.

Most of the song is verse. The words and the melody usually vary in this part of the song.

The chorus is the highlighted part of the song. The chorus is repeated, but its lyrics and melody stay the same throughout the song.

The **bridge** is a part of a song that is very different from the verse or chorus. It breaks up the song so that it is more interesting to listen to.

A typical rock song follows these patterns.

- Verse-chorus-verse-bridge-chorus. An example of this style is the song "My Generation," by the Who.

- Verse-bridge-verse. An example of this style is the song "Yesterday," by the Beatles.

9

Rock Instruments

A rock band usually uses three main instruments. They are a drum kit, an electric guitar, and a bass guitar. Sometimes a few other instruments are added as well.

Basic Rock Instruments

electric guitar

drum kit

bass guitar

Additional Instruments

keyboard

tambourine

harmonica

Rock Tools

Bands also need some tools that are not instruments to make rock music. Without these tools, you wouldn't be able to hear that rock sound.

Microphones. Microphones change the sounds from the singer and the drummer into electrical signals and feed them to the amplifiers.

Amplifiers. Amplifiers change electrical signals from the guitar and the microphones into loud sounds.

Guitar pedals. Guitar pedals are devices used to change the sound of a guitar. The different sounds are called effects.

Rock Greats

There are many well-known rock groups, musicians, and songs. Here is a list of just a few of the most popular rock greats.

Groups

- Aerosmith
- The Beach Boys
- The Beatles
- Blondie
- The Clash
- The Donnas
- Fleetwood Mac
- Kiss
- Led Zeppelin
- The Libertines
- Nirvana
- Pink Floyd
- The Police
- Pretenders
- The Rolling Stones
- Tegan and Sara
- U2
- The White Stripes

Musicians

- Chuck Berry
- Jimi Hendrix
- Chrissie Hynde
- Joan Jett
- Janis Joplin
- John Lennon
- Little Richard
- Paul McCartney
- Stevie Nicks
- Elvis Presley
- Prince
- Bonnie Raitt
- Patti Smith
- Stevie Wonder
- Tina Turner

Songs

- "Because the Night," by the Patti Smith Group
- "Blue Suede Shoes," performed by Elvis Presley
- "Heart of Glass," by Blondie
- "I Want to Hold Your Hand," by the Beatles
- "Purple Rain," by Prince
- "Seven Nation Army," by the White Stripes
- "Smells Like Teen Spirit," by Nirvana
- "Stairway to Heaven," by Led Zeppelin

Record Labels

A record label is a company that signs bands and then produces and sells their music. The name comes from the paper labels that are pasted in the center of vinyl records. These are some important record labels and the rock bands or musicians they signed.

- Sub Pop - signed Nirvana and Soundgarden
- Sun Records - discovered Elvis Presley, Johnny Cash, Carl Perkins, and Roy Orbison
- Atlantic Records - signed Led Zeppelin, the Melvins, and the Rolling Stones
- Columbia Records - signed David Bowie, Janis Joplin, and Pink Floyd
- Capitol Records - signed the Beatles, Pink Floyd, David Bowie, and the Red Hot Chili Peppers

Music Production

The way music is recorded makes a big difference in its final sound. The type of microphone used and where it is placed are very important. The **acoustics** in the recording room are critical.

Recording music is a difficult process. That is why most rock bands record in recording studios. A recording studio has professional recording equipment. It also has soundproof rooms. Studio engineers place the microphones and run the equipment.

Once the music is recorded, it needs to be worked with to bring out the best sound. This is mostly done with computer programs or mixing boards that help separate the sounds. This process is called mixing.

This sound engineer is using a mixing board.

Downloading Music

At one time, music could be bought only at record stores. Today you can buy music by downloading it onto your computer from a Web site. You can then put the downloaded music onto an MP3 player.

Sometimes people violate **copyright** law when they download music to their computers. Copyright law helps musicians get paid for their music. Some illegal Web sites let people download music without paying. You need to make sure you are downloading music from a legal Web site. Otherwise, you could be breaking copyright law.

It is also important that you get permission from an adult before downloading music. When you download music, you are charged a fee. Make sure an adult knows how much the music costs. And make sure an adult knows the Web site you are downloading from.

Record Collecting

Many people collect vinyl records. Music stores sell new and used records. You can also find used records at garage and estate sales. Many **audiophiles** prefer the sound of records. They believe the sound is warmer and truer than the sound of CDs.

Some musicians use parts of songs from old records to make new music. This is called sampling.

Experience Rock Music

There are many ways to listen to rock music. You can go to a live performance or listen to the radio. You can check out music at your local library or go to a rock music museum.

At many libraries, you can check out CDs and DVDs for free. You can watch concerts on DVDs, cable channels, and public television. Here are just a few ways you can experience and learn about rock music.

Concert Venues

Local newspapers usually list concerts. Look in the entertainment section for upcoming rock concerts. If you are under 18, the **venue** may require that you attend with an adult. Rock bands play at:

- community centers
- stadiums
- state fairs
- park bandstands
- art and music festivals
- theaters

Rock Museums

Rock museums are a great way to learn about the history of this music. You will learn about the bands and musicians that made rock so popular. Some museums are dedicated to rock. Other museums host traveling exhibits about rock music for a short time. Check your local newspaper for any rock music exhibits coming to your hometown.

Rock and Roll Hall of Fame and Museum

Cleveland, OH
www.rockhall.com

This museum **inducts** musicians into its Hall of Fame each year. The museum has exhibits, educational classes, and live performances.

Experience Music Project

Seattle, WA
www.empsfm.org

This museum covers the history of rock music. The exhibits are interactive and contain many types of rock **memorabilia**.

Memphis Rock 'n' Soul Museum

Memphis, TN
www.memphisrocknsoul.org

This museum was created with the Smithsonian Institution. It tells about the birth of rock and soul music.

Smithsonian National Museum of American History

Washington, DC
www.americanhistory.si.edu

There are several permanent exhibits about American music in this museum. They include sound recordings of Elvis Presley, photographs, and instruments.

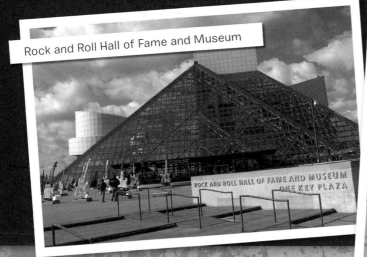

Rock and Roll Hall of Fame and Museum

Experience Music Project

Milk Carton
GUITAR

Guitars are an essential element of rock music. Try making this simple homemade guitar. You will need an adult helper with this project, so be sure to ask for help before starting.

Step 1

Trace the end of the yardstick onto the milk carton. Cut along the top and bottom lines of the tracing with the utility knife. Then cut a line through the middle to make an H shape. Repeat this on the opposite side of the milk carton.

Step 2

Slide the yardstick through the holes. One end should stick out farther than the other end.

Step 3

Cut a slot for each guitar string on the top of the milk carton. Try two or three strings to start. The top of the milk carton is the **bridge** of your guitar.

Step 4

Tack one end of each string to one end of the yardstick. Banjo strings come with loops in the ends. If you are using fishing line, you need to make the loops.

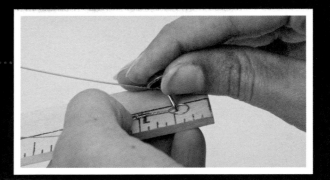

Step 5

Attach screw eyes to the other end of the yardstick. Stagger the screw eyes by an inch (2.5 cm). You will need one screw eye for each string.

Step 6

Push the strings securely into the slots and tightly tie each one to a screw eye. Turn the screw eyes to tighten the strings.

Step 7

Decorate your guitar! Cut out designs from construction paper and glue or tape them to the milk carton. Or, use markers to draw designs.

Playing Tips

- To change the sound of your strings, turn the screw eyes to tighten or loosen the strings.

- Try plucking and strumming the strings for different sounds.

- Experiment with the sound by playing the strings on both sides of the **bridge**.

- Hold the strings down so they touch the yardstick and pluck the strings. When you hear a sound you like, mark that place on the yardstick. This will make it easier to find the sounds that you like!

- Take the cap off of the milk carton to hear how it affects the sound.

ROCK to the BEAT

The beat is what holds music together. Here are two common rock beats that you can make by clapping your hands or stomping your feet. Or, you can improvise and make a drum and drumsticks out of things you can find in your house.

Basic Rock Beat

To make this beat, first try clapping out each number. Next, while clapping out the beat, stomp at the stressed beats, which are beats 2 and 4. This will make a louder sound. If you are using a drum and drumsticks, use both sticks on the stressed beats.

Count out this beat:

1 & 2 & 3 & 4 & 1 & 2 & 3 & 4 &

Now do it again but stress the bold beats:

1 & **2** & 3 & **4** & 1 & **2** & 3 & **4** &

The Rock Triplet

To make this beat, clap or beat a drum in three quick beats. Pause after the third beat. Then repeat the triplet.

1 2 3   1 2 3   1 2 3   1 2 3   1 2 3   1 2 3

CLEF NOTES

A drum solo is when the drums are louder than the other instruments. The other musicians stop playing or play softly during a drum solo. Then the drummer shows off his or her skills on the drums!

Found-Object Percussion

If you don't have drums to play, try using these household items instead!

coffee can

plastic milk container

pencils

chopsticks

Write a
ROCK SONG

Materials Needed

- notebook and pencil
- tape recorder
- any instruments you want to use

Putting together a simple song is not as hard as it seems. It can be as simple or as complicated as you want it to be. There are basic song elements that you can use to create your own song.

Lyrics tell the story of the song. They usually contain three parts, the verse, the **bridge**, and the chorus.

A melody is a sequence of notes that are played on an instrument, sung, or hummed.

The beat holds the song together. It needs to be steady so the melody and lyrics have something to follow.

Rock Lyrics

1 Rock **lyrics** can tell a story or describe a feeling or an emotion. A basic rock song has a repeating chorus, which usually contains the title of the song. The verses tell the story or describe the emotion. The **bridge** breaks up the song. Bridge lyrics are different from the verse and the chorus but should relate to the main idea.

2 Pick a story you want to tell. You can tell about a day at school or something you did with your friends. Write down the main idea of the song and turn that into the title.

3 Make a list of things you want to include in your lyrics. Don't think too much, just let your ideas flow!

4 Next, start writing! For your chorus, you can think of two to three lines that tell the main emotion of your story.

5 Then write a couple of verses that tell the listener your story. Your lyrics can rhyme at the end of each phrase or not. Try to tell how you felt about what happened in your story. Remember, music is all about emotion!

6 Finally, write the bridge. This part can show up once or a few times in the song.

Sample Lyrics

Chorus:

School can be tough, oh yeah
Sometimes it's rough, yeah yeah

Verse:

I was in class one day
and the teacher said to me
"Stop your daydreaming!"
as I sat staring out the window
at a tree.

Bridge:

While that day was hard,
it taught me to see
that listening at school
is probably good for me!

Cool Rock Phrases

- Oh, yeah
- Hey, babe
- My mama says

- Baby, baby, baby
- Come on
- I got a feeling

Rock Melody

1 The melody is a series of notes that you think sound good together. Try to find those notes by experimenting with your instrument. Also, sing your lyrics while playing your instrument to hear which melody works best.

2 Choose an instrument and try to play a melody on it. Choose three notes that you think sound good together. Create a pattern for your notes. For example, you could play one note for the first three beats and a different note for the fourth beat. Practice playing the pattern over and over.

CLEF NOTES

The simplest of melodies use just a few notes! Listen to these rock songs. Notice how simple the melodies are.

- "Let it be," by the Beatles
- "Do You Remember Rock 'N' Roll Radio," by the Ramones

3 Next, start singing! Experiment with how your lyrics and your melody work together. Set one style for the verse, one for the chorus, and another for the bridge. Tape-record your melody and lyrics. After trying different **versions**, pick your favorite. Have fun and try to keep it simple!

Put Your Song Together!

1 Ask a friend to play the drums in the basic rock beat. Or, record yourself playing the drumbeat. Play the basic rock beat for two minutes. Then rewind the tape and get ready to play your melody.

2 Next, play your melody while you play back the recording of your beat.

3 Finally, start from the top. Sing your **lyrics** and play the melody while the recorded beat plays.

4 Now that you've put it all together, use a tape recorder to record your song. Have a friend play the drums while you play the melody and sing the lyrics. Then you can listen to how all the parts sound together.

CLEF NOTES

Very few songs start off sounding great! It is very important to practice your song many times. The more you play it, the more your song will change and improve.

Cool Rock
DANCES

Materials Needed

- stereo
- "The Twist," by Chubby Checker, for the first dance and any rock song you like for the second dance

As rock music became popular in the 1950s, people created special dance steps for certain songs. Today people usually make up their own style of dancing for rock music. This is called freestyle dancing, which means that it is made up on the spot. Here are examples of both types of rock dancing. Let's rock!

The Twist

1 Stand with one foot ahead of the other. Now start moving the foot that is forward in a twisting motion. Be sure to keep the ball of your foot on the floor.

2 Next, pretend you are holding a towel behind your back. Imagine you have one end of the towel in each hand. Pull the pretend towel from side to side.

3 Try bending forward and leaning back while doing all these movements together. Now you're twisting!

Freestyle Dance

1 First, pick how you want to move the bottom half of your body to the beat. You can sway from left to right, jump up and down, or do little kicks forward. Choose whatever movement is the most fun for you.

2 Next, pick a way to move your arms and hands. You can lift your elbows up to the sides. You can swing your arms forward and snap your fingers. You can even move your arms in all different directions.

3 Now add your head. Try bobbing it up and down or swinging it from side to side. Just keep moving to the beat and create your own freestyle dance!

Make a ROCK VIDEO

Materials Needed

- song and lyrics
- stereo or MP3 player
- props to create an image
- guitar
- drums
- broom to use as a microphone stand
- video camera

Some rock videos are like short plays that tell the story of the song. Others just show the band playing the song. This kind of video usually has a lot of close-up shots of the band members. But both kinds of videos are fun to make!

Step 1

Pick the song you want to play in your rock video. Find the **lyrics** online and print them out. Or, just pretend you know the lyrics when you perform the song. Recruit some friends to play the other members of the group.

Step 2

Create an image for your band. Either copy the band's look or create your own funky style. Decide whether you want to tell a story or just play the song in the video. Decide how you will dress. Create a dance move that all band members will do.

Step 3

Practice your song and dance move. When you are ready to perform, ask your friends or family to gather and watch. Ask someone to record your performance. Set up the song on the stereo or the MP3 player. Get dressed for the part and then have fun performing the song!

Conclusion

Rock music can be fun to listen to. And it can be even more fun to play!

As you listen to more rock bands, you will learn about the different styles of rock. This will inspire you when you try to make your own rock music. Be patient while you practice your music, because you will only improve with time. Also, remember to let yourself experiment with the sound. This is how all great musicians find their unique styles.

If you are a collector, try listening to all kinds of rock music. You will be surprised at what you discover you like. Have fun with your collection and find music that expresses your musical style.

Music is something that everyone can enjoy, whether they are musicians, music lovers, or both! Just remember to have fun and rock on!

Glossary

acoustic – being an instrument that does not need to be amplified.

acoustics – the properties of a room that affect how sound is heard in it.

audience – a group of people watching a performance.

audiophile – a person who is very enthusiastic about listening to recorded music.

bridge – the part of a song that links sections of a song; the part of a stringed instrument that raises the strings.

copyright – the legal right to copy, sell, publish, or distribute the work of a writer, musician, or artist.

genre – a category of art, music, or literature.

induct – to admit someone as a member.

lyrics – the words of a song.

memorabilia – an item that serves as a remembrance of a person or an event.

tempo - the speed at which a piece of music is played.

venue – a place where specific kinds of events take place.

version – a different form or type of the original.

Web Sites

To learn more about cool music, visit ABDO Publishing Company on the World Wide Web at **www.abdopublishing.com**. Web sites about cool music are featured on our Book Links pages. These links are routinely monitored and updated to provide the most current information available.

Index